The Thai Book of Soup Goodness

The Most Mouthwatering Thai Soup Recipes for Soup Lovers

By

Angel Burns

© 2019 Angel Burns, All Rights Reserved.

License Notices

This book or parts thereof might not be reproduced in any format for personal or commercial use without the written permission of the author. Possession and distribution of this book by any means without said permission is prohibited by law.

All content is for entertainment purposes and the author accepts no responsibility for any damages, commercially or personally, caused by following the content.

Table of Contents

Mouthwatering Thai Soup Recipes 6

Recipe 1: Thai Sour Soup 7

Recipe 2: Thai Milk Vegetables and Coconut Soup 9

Recipe 3: Thai Noodles Soup 12

Recipe 4: Tom Yum Soup 15

Recipe 5: Gai Tom Kha Namsai Soup 18

Recipe 6: Thai Wonton Soup 20

Recipe 7: Thai Poultry Soup 23

Recipe 8: Thai Chicken Noodles Soup 25

Recipe 9: Seafood Tamarind Soup 28

Recipe 10: Chicken Noodle Soup with Lemongrass 30

Recipe 11: Mustard Greens Soup 33

Recipe 12: Coconut Pumpkin Soup 35

Recipe 13: Pork and Cabbage Soup 38

Recipe 14: Veggie Tom Yum Soup 41

Recipe 15: Thai Vegetable Stew 44

Recipe 16: Hot and Sour Soup 47

Recipe 17: No-Noodle Chicken Soup 50

Recipe 18: Tom Ka Gai Soup 53

Recipe 19: Spicy Mushroom Soup 56

Recipe 20: Orange Fish Soup 58

Recipe 21: Thai Sweet and Sour Chicken Soup 61

Recipe 22: Shrimp and Pumpkin Thai Soup 63

Recipe 23: Thai Vegetable Soup 66

Recipe 24: Thai Carrot Soup 69

Recipe 25: Chicken Ginger Soup 72

Recipe 26: Traditional Tom Yum 75

Recipe 27: Five Spice Soup 78

Recipe 28: Thai Seafood Soup 81

Recipe 29: Rice Shrimp Soup 84

[4]

Recipe 30: Tom Yum in Coconut Water with Shrimp.. 87

About the Author 90

Author's Afterthoughts... 92

Mouthwatering Thai Soup Recipes

HHHHHHHHHHHHHHHHHHHHHHHHHHHHHHH

Recipe 1: Thai Sour Soup

This soup is aromatic with turmeric zest.

Preparation Time: 20 mins

Yield: 8

Ingredient List:

- 2 Pounds Chicken, pieces
- 8-9 Cups Chicken Stock
- 3-4 Stalks Fresh Lemongrass, pieces
- 3-4 turmeric slices, chopped
- 5-6 Cloves of Garlic, crushed
- 10-12 Kaffir Lime Leaves
- ¼ Cup Tamarind Paste

HHHHHHHHHHHHHHHHHHHHHHHHHHHHHH

Instructions:

1. Add chicken stock in a pot, let to boil.

2. Add in lemongrass, galangal, turmeric paste, chopped turmeric, garlic and kefir lime leaves. Boil for 30 minutes on low flame.

Recipe 2: Thai Milk Vegetables and Coconut Soup

This soup is great combination of vegetables and coconut milk.

Preparation Time: 20 mins

Yield: 4

Ingredient List:

- 1 Cup Coconut Milk
- ½ Cup Peas
- ½ Cup Beans
- 1 Cup Mushrooms, Sliced
- ½ Cup Cabbage, chopped
- 2 Shallots, sliced
- 2 tsp. Light Soy Sauce
- 2 tsp. Palm Sugar
- 2 tbsp. Red Thai Chiles, Sliced
- 2 tbsp. Green Peppercorns
- 5 Lime Leaves, shredded
- 2 carrots, peeled, sliced
- 1 block of tofu, sliced

HHHHHHHHHHHHHHHHHHHHHHHHHHHHHH

Instructions:

1. In a saucepan add in coconut milk and simmer.

2. Add in sugar, soy sauce and lime leaves.

3. Add in shallots and pepper, cook for 1-2 minutes.

4. Add in vegetables and tofu, boil for few minutes.

5. Serve with noodles.

Recipe 3: Thai Noodles Soup

You love to have noodle soup? Today make is in Thai style.

Preparation Time: 30 mins

Yield: 3

Ingredient List:

- 6 cups chicken broth
- 2 chicken breasts, pieces
- 2 stalks of lemongrass, chopped
- 4 cloves garlic, minced
- 2 tbsp. lime juice
- 2 tbsp. fish sauce
- ¼ cup coconut milk
- Some black pepper
- Cilantro, for garnish
- Spring onion, for garnish
- 1 package Thai rice noodles, boiled
- Salt, to taste

HHHHHHHHHHHHHHHHHHHHHHHHHHHHHHH

Instructions:

1. In a saucepan add chicken stock, garlic, and lemongrass.

2. Add inch chicken and cook for 6-7 minutes on high flame.

3. Add in lime juice, fish sauce, pepper, and some salt.

4. Now add coconut milk and simmer on low heat for 3-4 minutes.

5. Now ladle soup in bowl with noodles.

6. Top with coriander and spring onion.

Recipe 4: Tom Yum Soup

This Thai soup is going to be sour new friend.

Preparation Time: 30 mins

Yield: 2

Ingredient List:

- 3 cups chicken stock
- 1-2 stalk lemongrass, chopped
- 3-4 cloves garlic, chopped minced
- 1 tsp. crushed chili, dried
- 4 kaffir lime leaves
- ½ cup shiitake mushrooms, sliced
- 16 shrimps
- 1 green bell pepper, sliced
- some cherry tomatoes, optional
- ¼ can coconut milk
- 3 tbsp. fish sauce
- 2 tsp. brown sugar
- Coriander, for garnish

HHHHHHHHHHHHHHHHHHHHHHHHHHHHHH

Instructions:

1. In a pot add chicken broth and let to boil on high flame.

2. Add in lemongrass and cook for 5-6 minutes.

3. Now add garlic, chili, mushrooms, kefir lime leaves, cook on low heat for 4 minutes.

4. Add shrimp, sliced bell pepper, and all cherry tomatoes, let to boil for 5-6 minutes.

5. Add in coconut milk and 2 tsp. of fish sauce. Add in brown sugar and simmer for 1-2 minutes.

6. Transfer to serving bowls and top with coriander.

Recipe 5: Gai Tom Kha Namsai Soup

A new version of Thai soup is waiting for you.

Preparation Time: 40 mins

Yield: 4

Ingredient List:

- 5 Cups Water
- 2 Pound Chicken, Cut into piece
- 2-3 inch Fresh Galangal, Sliced
- 1 tbsp. Salt
- 1 tbsp. Spring Onion
- 1 tbsp. Cilantro

Instructions:

1. In a soup pan add water and let it to boil.

2. Add in chicken and cook on low flame for 9-10 minutes.

3. Add galangal, and salt, cook for another 30 minutes.

4. Transfer soup in serving bowls.

5. Top with spring onion and cilantro.

6. Enjoy.

Recipe 6: Thai Wonton Soup

This soup is best for your whole family members specially your children.

Preparation Time: 40 mins

Yield: 6

Ingredient List:

- 6-7 cups of broth chicken
- 1 lemongrass stalk, chopped
- 3-5 mushrooms, slicked
- 1 tbsp. soy sauce
- 1 cup chicken, boneless, boiled
- 3 tsp. ginger, grated
- 2 spring onions, sliced
- 1 tsp. oyster sauce
- 2 tbsp. fish sauce
- Optional: one red chili, sliced
- 1 small cucumber, sliced
- 1 tbsp. lime juice
- 1 package of wonton wrappers
- Coriander and onion, for garnish

HHHHHHHHHHHHHHHHHHHHHHHHHHHHHH

Instructions:

1. In a food processor add chicken, ginger, fish sauce, spring onions, and oyster sauce, press.

2. Spread wonton wrappers and brush them with some water.

3. Place 1-2 tsp. of mixture at the center each wrapper and fold the corner up to make dumpling shape.

4. In a pot add chicken broth and let to boil it on high flame.

5. Add in the lemongrass, soy sauce, and slice mushrooms. Let to boil.

6. After that simmer for 5 minutes.

7. Put dumplings in chicken broth with chili. Cook for 5 minutes.

8. Reduce the flame and add in cucumbers.

9. Drizzle lime juice.

10. When done ladle soup in bowls. Garnish with coriander and spring onion.

Recipe 7: Thai Poultry Soup

Enjoy making this soup and share with your loved ones.

Preparation Time: 45 mins

Yield: 4

Ingredient List:

- ½ Duck or chicken, pieces
- 4-6 Cups Water
- 20-22 Black Peppercorns, crushed
- 6 Cloves Garlic, minced
- 3 tbsp. coriander seeds, crushed
- 1 melon, sliced
- 1-2 Pickled Lime, sliced
- 4 Tbsp. Soy Sauce
- ½ Tsp. Salt
- 5 Spring Onions, sliced
- Vegetable Oil for frying

HHHHHHHHHHHHHHHHHHHHHHHHHHHHHHH

Instructions:

1. In a saucepan add plenty of water and let to boil.

2. Add in duck and let to simmer for 30 minutes.

3. Now add in garlic, peppercorn, and coriander.

4. Add in all remaining Ingredients, simmer for another 30 minutes.

5. Enjoy hot.

Recipe 8: Thai Chicken Noodles Soup

Make this new version of soup and give your loved ones a real treat.

Preparation Time: 35 mins

Yield: 6

Ingredient List:

- 7 cups chicken broth
- 3 fresh chicken breasts, cut into pieces
- 2 small stalks lemongrass , chopped
- 5 kaffir lime leaves
- 1-inch ginger slice, chopped
- 1 carrot, sliced
- 4-5 baby bok choy bushes, chopped
- 1 red chili, chopped
- 3-6 cloves garlic, minced
- 1/3 cup fresh lime juice
- 2 tbsp. fish sauce
- ¼ cup coconut milk
- Black pepper, to taste
- ¼ cup cilantro
- 81 package of Thai noodles, boiled

HHHHHHHHHHHHHHHHHHHHHHHHHHHHHH

Instructions:

1. In a soup pot add chicken stock and let to boil

2. Add in fresh, lemongrass, ginger, boy choy, carrot, and lime leaves. Let to boil.

3. Now reduce flame and let to cook covered for 5-6 minutes.

4. Now add in chili, chopped garlic, oyster sauce, lime juice, and fish sauce. Mix well.

5. Now drizzle coconut milk, mix well.

6. Add some noodles in serving bowls, drizzle soup.

7. Serve with coriander.

Recipe 9: Seafood Tamarind Soup

This is simple soup with allots of nutrients.

Preparation Time: 35 mins

Yield: 4

Ingredient List:

- 1-2 Pound Cod
- 6-8 Prawns
- 3 Spring Onion, sliced
- 2-3 Thai Chili, sliced
- 3 Tbsp. Onion, sliced
- 2 Tsp. Fish Sauce
- 2 Tsp. Tamarind Paste
- Salt and pepper, to taste

HHHHHHHHHHHHHHHHHHHHHHHHHHHHHHH

Instructions:

1. In a soup pot add fish, sliced green onion, onion, pepper, salt, Thai chili pepper, and about 6 cups of water. Cook for 20 minutes on medium heat.

2. Now add in handful of green vegetables and stir to combine.

3. Enjoy.

Recipe 10: Chicken Noodle Soup with Lemongrass

Do you love the aroma of Lemongrass? Add it in your soup bowl and enjoy the real flavor.

Preparation Time: 30 mins

Yield: 3

Ingredient List:

- 1 package of egg noodles, boiled
- 6-7 cups chicken stock
- 1 lemongrass, chopped
- ½ pounds of chicken boneless, cut into strips
- 4 lime leaves
- 3-4 garlic cloves, minced
- 1-2-inch piece ginger, grated
- 1 chili, sliced
- 1 carrot, sliced
- 1 celery stick, sliced
- 1 tbsp. oyster sauce
- ½ tbsp. sugar
- 3 tbsp. fish sauce
- 2 cups baby bok choy, chopped
- 1 cup coconut milk
- coriander, for garnish

HHHHHHHHHHHHHHHHHHHHHHHHHHHHHHH

Instructions:

1. In a soup pan add chicken stock and let to boil.

2. Add in lime leaves with chicken and boil for 3-4 minutes.

3. Now add in garlic, ginger, red chili, carrot, and chopped celery. Cook for 3-4 minutes.

4. Now add oyster sauce, bok choy, fish sauce as and sugar. Simmer for 30 seconds.

5. Now add in coconut milk and mix on low flame.

6. Transfer cooked noodles in serving bowls and top with hot soup

7. Sprinkle coriander on top.

Recipe 11: Mustard Greens Soup

This is a real simple soup packed with flavors.

Preparation Time: 45 mins

Yield: 4

Ingredient List:

- 1 Pork bone
- 1 Package Mustard Green
- 2 Tbsp. Thin Soy Sauce
- Salt and pepper, to taste
- 2-3 garlic cloves, minced

HHHHHHHHHHHHHHHHHHHHHHHHHHHHHHH

Instructions:

1. In a soup pot add all Ingredients and let to boil on high flame.

2. Now reduce heat and cook covered for 30-35 minutes.

3. Enjoy hot.

Recipe 12: Coconut Pumpkin Soup

This creamy and mouth melting soup is a great blessing.

Preparation Time: 35mins

Yield: 3

Ingredient List:

- 7 cups chicken stock
- 1/3 can thick coconut milk
- 4 tbsp. lemongrass
- 4 kaffir lime leaves
- 3 ½ cups pumpkin, chunks
- 2 cups yam, peeled, chunks
- 1 cup tofu, sliced,
- 1 shallot, minced
- 3-4 cloves garlic, minced
- 1-inch ginger, slice
- 1 fresh red chili, sliced
- ½ tsp. turmeric
- 3 tsp. coriander powder
- 1 tsp. cumin powder
- 2 tbsp. fish sauce
- ½ tsp. shrimp paste
- 1 tsp. brown sugar
- 2 tbsp. lime juice
- 1 handful baby spinach
- ½ cup basil, for garnish

HHHHHHHHHHHHHHHHHHHHHHHHHHHHH

Instructions:

1. In a pot add stock and let to boil on high flame.

2. Add in lemongrass, kaffir lime leaves, shallot, minced garlic, ginger, and chopped chili. Let to boil well.

3. Add in pumpkin and yam, boil for 6-8 minutes on low heat.

4. Now add turmeric, coriander powder, cumin, brown sugar, fish sauce, shrimp paste, and lime juice.

5. Now add in coconut milk and let to boil on low heat.

6. Add tofu and spinach and mix it.

7. Serve with noodles in bowls and top with basil and coriander.

Recipe 13: Pork and Cabbage Soup

This soup is not only simple to make but delicious to taste.

Preparation Time: 35 mins

Yield: 4

Ingredient List:

- 8-10 Cups Water
- 2 Pound Ground Pork
- 2 Tsp. Coriander Seed
- 4-5 Cloves Garlic
- 1 Tsp. Thai Pepper
- 1 Head of Cabbage, sliced
- 2 Tsp. Salt
- 6 Tsp. Soy Sauce
- 5 Tsp. Sugar
- 2 Tbsp. Preserved Cabbage

HHHHHHHHHHHHHHHHHHHHHHHHHHHHHHH

Instructions:

1. Press the pepper powder with garlic and coriander in the mortar and pestle.

2. Transfer this mixture in ground pork, with soy sauce, toss to combine.

3. In a soup pot add water and let boil.

4. Meanwhile add in pork, cabbage, add preserved cabbage. Cook for 20-minutes on low heat.

5. Season with salt, sugar and some Thai pepper powder.

6. Transfer to serving dish and garnish with cilantro and spring onion.

Recipe 14: Veggie Tom Yum Soup

This clearing soup can be served with plain rice or with bread.

Preparation Time: 35 mins

Yield: 4

Ingredient List:

- 1 stalk lemongrass, minced
- 5 cups chicken stock
- 1 red chili, sliced
- 4 kaffir lime leaves
- 1-inch ginger piece, sliced
- 4 garlic cloves, minced
- 1 cup baby bok choy, chopped
- 1 cup mushrooms, sliced
- ½ can good-quality coconut milk, optional
- 1 cup cherry tomatoes
- 3 tbsp. soy sauce
- 1 tsp. brown sugar
- 1 cup soft tofu, sliced
- 1 tbsp. lime juice
- ¼ cup coriander, chopped
- ¼ cup basil, chopped

Instructions:

1. Add chicken stock in a saucepan and let to boil,

2. Add in lemongrass, lime leaves, chili, minced garlic, ginger. Boil well for 4-5 minutes.

3. Add in mushrooms. Reduce flame and cook mushrooms for 6-7 minutes.

4. Add bok choy with cherry tomatoes, simmer 1-2 more minutes

5. Now reduce flame and mix in sugar, soy sauce, and fresh lime juice.

6. Stir in soft tofu.

7. Ladle soup in serving bowls and sprinkle basil and coriander.

Recipe 15: Thai Vegetable Stew

Blow the mind of your loved ones with this hot bowl of soup.

Preparation Time: 35 mins

Yield: 4

Ingredient List:

- 1 Pound Pork, pieces
- ½ Chicken, pieces
- 4-5 Cups Radish, peeled, sliced
- 1 cup Cabbage, chunks
- 2 cup Western Cabbage, pieces
- 2 Cup Leeks, cut into pieces
- 3 Cups Celery, pieces
- 3 Cups Kale, chopped
- 10-12 Chinese Mushrooms, sliced
- 5 Cakes of Tofu, quartered, cut into pieces
- 3 Cups Thread Noodles
- ¼ Cup Coriander chopped
- 10 tsp. Soybean Paste
- 4 Tbsp. Chopped Garlic
- 1 Tbsp. Ginger, minced
- 3 Tbsp. Fish Sauce
- 2 Tbsp. Dark Soy Sauce
- 2 Tbsp. Maggi Sauce
- 3 Tbsp. Palm Sugar
- 8-10 Cups Pork Stock

HHHHHHHHHHHHHHHHHHHHHHHHHHHHH

Instructions:

1. In a saucepan add pork, pork stock, poultry, fish sauce, soy sauce, and Maggi sauce, let to boil well.

2. Add in all vegetables, tofu, and noodles.

3. In a separate pan heat some oil and cook soybean paste till fragrant. Add in garlic and ginger. Stir this mixture int soup pot. Stir well.

4. Enjoy hot.

Recipe 16: Hot and Sour Soup

Do you love a hot and spicy flavor? Make your soup in this way.

Preparation Time: 50 mins

Yield: 4

Ingredient List:

- 1 block of tofu, cut into pieces
- 1 ½ pounds pork tenderloin
- 1 cup bamboo shoots
- 2 tbsp. black fungus, soaked in water
- 1 handful of lily buds, soaked in water
- 6-7 cups water
- 1 tsp. salt
- 1 tsp. sugar
- 2 tbsp. soy sauce
- 2 tbsp. rice vinegar
- 1 tsp. sesame oil
- 1 tbsp. Cornstarch, dissolve it in 4 tbsp. of water
- 1 egg, whisked
- 1 green onion, chopped
- White pepper to taste

HHHHHHHHHHHHHHHHHHHHHHHHHHHHHH

Instructions:

1. Shred pork.

2. Marinate pork in soya sauce for 20 minutes.

3. In a saucepan add water and let it to boil.

4. Add in bamboo shoots, fungus and lily buds.

5. Add tofu and marinated pork. Let to boil

6. Now mix in salt, sugar, some more soy sauce, vinegar and sesame oil.

7. Drizzle corn flour mixture in soup and stir well. Let to boil for 1 minute.

8. Now add in egg and mix.

9. Add in green onion and pepper.

10. Enjoy.

Recipe 17: No-Noodle Chicken Soup

Making this soup is a real magic.

Preparation Time: 30 mins

Yield: 4

Ingredient List:

- 2 ½ ounces butter
- 1-2 celery stalk
- 3-4 ounces of mushrooms, chopped
- 1 garlic clove, minced
- 1 tbsp. onion, minced
- 1 tsp. parsley
- 5 cups chicken broth
- 1 carrot, peeled, sliced
- 1 cup chicken, shredded
- 1 ¼ cup green cabbage
- Salt and pepper to taste

HHHHHHHHHHHHHHHHHHHHHHHHHHHHHHH

Instructions:

1. Melt butter and in a pan and cook add onion with celery stalks.

2. Now add in mushrooms and minced garlic. Stir fry for 5 minutes.

3. Add in broth, carrots and parsley.

4. Season with salt and pepper.

5. Cook until vegetables are tendered.

6. Now add in shredded chicken and mix well.

7. Simmer for 10-15 minutes.

8. Enjoy.

Recipe 18: Tom Ka Gai Soup

Are you looking for a bowl of soup which can please you till soul? Then you found it here.

Preparation Time: 25 mins

Yield: 2

Ingredient List:

- 1 stalk lemongrass, chopped
- 6-7 cups chicken stock
- 2-3 chicken breasts, sliced
- 1 cup mushrooms, sliced
- 3 kaffir limes leaves
- 1 to 2 red chilies, chopped
- 1-piece ginger, chopped
- ½ can coconut milk
- 2 tbsp. fish sauce
- 2 tbsp. lime juice
- 1 tsp. brown sugar
- Some coriander leaves
- Some basil leaves
- 3 spring onions, sliced

HHHHHHHHHHHHHHHHHHHHHHHHHHHHHH

Instructions:

1. Transfer lemongrass in soup pot with chicken broth. Let to boil.

2. Add chicken, mushrooms, kaffir lime leaves, and chilies. Cook for 5-6 minutes.

3. Now add ginger, coconut milk, sugar, the fish sauce, simmer for 1-2 minutes.

4. Add lime juice and mix.

5. Ladle soup in serving bowls.

6. Top with coriander, basil, and spring onions.

Recipe 19: Spicy Mushroom Soup

You will feel loved after trying this soup.

Preparation Time: 5 mins

Yield: 4

Ingredient List:

- 2 Pounds Mushrooms, sliced
- 4 Cups Water
- 1-2 Lemongrass Stalk, sliced
- 3 slices of Galangal, chopped
- 3-4 Kaffir Lime Leaves
- 3 Tbsp. Soy Sauce
- 3-4 Tbsp. Lime Juice
- 10-12 Whole Dried Chile Peppers
- 1-2 Spring Onion, Chopped

HHHHHHHHHHHHHHHHHHHHHHHHHHHHHHH

Instructions:

1. Ina saucepan add water and let it to boil

2. Add in galaga, lemongrass, kefir lime leaves and mushrooms. Let to cook until mushrooms are softened.

3. Add in soy sauce, lime juice, Chile peppers.

4. Top with spring onion while serving.

5. Enjoy.

Recipe 20: Orange Fish Soup

This orange zest fish soup is going to be your loved one.

Preparation Time: 25 mins

Yield: 2

Ingredient List:

- 6 cups chicken stock
- 2-4 fillets of sole, cut into pieces
- 10-12 shrimp
- 1 cup orange juice
- 3 tsp. tamarind paste
- 1 tbsp. palm sugar
- 3 tbsp. fish sauce
- 2 ½ cups baby bok choy, chopped
- 1 cup cherry tomatoes
- 1 cup green beans, chopped
- 1 zucchini, chopped
- 4-5 orange slices

For the Paste:

- 1 shallot, chopped
- ½ red chili
- 1-inch piece ginger
- 3-4 cloves garlic
- ½ tsp. white pepper
- 1 tsp. shrimp paste
- 1 tbsp. fish sauce
- handful of coriander

Instructions:

1. add paste Ingredients in food processor and press well. Asset aside.

2. In a soup pot heat oil and add in paste, stir for 1-2 minutes.

3. Stir in stock, orange juice, sugar, tamarind pulp, and sugar, let to boil.

4. Add in beans and cook for 4-5 minutes.

5. Add in all remaining vegetables with fish and shrimp. Cook for 2 to 3 minutes.

6. Now add fish sauce.

7. Ladle soup in bowls.

8. Top with orange slices and fresh coriander.

Recipe 21: Thai Sweet and Sour Chicken Soup

Sweet and soup Thai soup is one of the famous soup.

Preparation Time: 30 mins

Yield: 4

Ingredient List:

- 2 pounds chicken, bite size pieces
- 5 Cups Chicken Stock
- 2 Tbsp. Sesame Oil
- 1 tsp. Ginger, Ground
- 3 Tbsp. Sour Curry Paste
- 4 tbsp. Fish Sauce
- 2 Tbsp. Tamarind pulp
- 3 Tbsp. Palm Sugar
- 2-3 Cups Green Vegetables, chopped
- 1 Cup Pineapple, Chunks

HHHHHHHHHHHHHHHHHHHHHHHHHHHHHH

Instructions:

1. In a bowl add chicken, sesame oil and ginger. Marinade for 1 hour.

2. Now heat a pan and fry the chicken until no longer pink.

3. Add in stock and all Ingredients pineapple, cook for few minutes.

4. Now add in pineapple and mix well.

5. Serve hot.

Recipe 22: Shrimp and Pumpkin Thai Soup

This soup is going to give you unforgettable taste.

Preparation Time: 20 mins

Yield: 2

Ingredient List:

- 6 cups chicken stock
- 4 cups pumpkin, chunks
- 1-2 cups sweet potato, cubed
- 12-16 tiger prawns
- 2 heads of baby bok choy, sliced
- 1/3 can coconut milk
- 2-4 kaffir lime leaves
- 1 stalk lemongrass, minced
- 3-4 cloves garlic, minced
- 1 shallot, minced
- 1-inch ginger slice, minced
- ½ tsp. chili powder
- 1 tsp. ground coriander
- 1 tsp. ground cumin
- 3 tbsp. fish sauce
- ½ tsp. turmeric powder
- 1 tsp. brown sugar
- 1 tbsp. lime juice
- 1 red chili, sliced
- Some fresh coriander

Instructions:

1. In a saucepan add stock with lemon grass, lime leaves, garlic, chopped shallot, or ginger and boil for 1-2 minutes.

2. Add in pumpkin and sweet potato. Let to boil for 5-6 minutes.

3. Now add in prawns, bok choy, chili powder, coriander, lime juice, cumin, turmeric, fish sauce, shrimp paste, brown sugar, and chili. Cook for 3 minutes.

4. Now add in coconut milk and simmer for 3 minutes.

5. Ladle soup in bowls and top with coriander.

Recipe 23: Thai Vegetable Soup

This vegetable soup is going to blow your mind.

Preparation Time: 35 mins

Yield: 4

Ingredient List:

- 10-12 Black Peppercorns
- 2 tsp. Shrimp Paste
- 4 Tbsp. Fish Sauce
- 10-12 Shallots, chopped
- 10-12 Shrimps
- 2 tsp. Red Curry Paste
- 2-3 Tbsp. Chili Paste
- 2 Tbsp. Fish Sauce
- 5-6 Cups mixed Vegetables
- 5-6 Stems of Fresh Thai Basil
- 5 Cups Vegetable Stock

HHHHHHHHHHHHHHHHHHHHHHHHHHHHHHH

Instructions:

1. In a food processor add last 6 Ingredients and process until fine paste is made.

2. Add stock in saucepan and let to boil.

3. Add in spice paste, Thai curry paste, and shrimp paste, and stir well.

4. Add the fish sauce and all vegetables plus basil, cook until vegetables are softened.

5. Enjoy hot.

Recipe 24: Thai Carrot Soup

Thai Carrot soup is magic in your bowl.

Preparation Time: 30 mins

Yield: 4

Ingredient List:

- 2 tbsp. oil
- 1 small onion, chopped
- 3 cloves garlic, chopped
- 1 stalk lemongrass, chopped
- 1 red chili, minced
- 4 cups broth
- ½ cup Thai jasmine rice
- 7 carrots, sliced
- 1 tbsp. Cumin powder
- ¼ tsp. cardamom powder
- ¼ tsp. nutmeg
- 1 can coconut milk
- 2 tbsp. fish sauce
- ½ lime, juiced
- 1 tbsp. soy sauce
- 1 handful coriander
- 1 handful basil

HHHHHHHHHHHHHHHHHHHHHHHHHHHHHH

Instructions:

1. In a soup pan add in oil and cook onion, garlic, ginger, lemongrass and chili, stir-fry for 1 minute.

2. Add in broth let to boil.

3. Add in carrots with rice and all spices.

4. Lower the heat and cook for 15 minutes.

5. Add in coconut milk and mix.

6. Now puree the soup with beater.

7. Pour soup again in soup pan and let to warm.

8. Add in fish sauce, soy sauce and lime juice.

9. Ladle in serving bowls and top with coriander and basil.

Recipe 25: Chicken Ginger Soup

Ginger is going to make this soup a real delight.

Preparation Time: 40 mins

Yield: 4

Ingredient List:

- 2 tbsp. Vegetable Oil
- 2 Cups Chicken, bite size
- 6-7 cloves of Garlic, crushed
- 3 tbsp. Ginger, sliced
- 2 Tbsp. Bean Sauce
- 3 Cups Water
- ½ Tbsp. Soy Sauce
- ½ Tsp. Thai Powder
- ¼ Cup Spring Onion, sliced
- 2 Tbsp. Cilantro, chopped
- Thai chilies, for garnish

HHHHHHHHHHHHHHHHHHHHHHHHHHHHHH

Instructions:

1. Heat oil in a pan and fry chicken until lightly golden.

2. Now add in add garlic and ginger stir fry for 1-2 minutes.

3. Add yellow bean sauce and water, let to boil for 5-6 minutes.

4. Now add soy sauce and white pepper.

5. Add in spring onion and cilantro.

6. Put to serving bowls and top with Thai chilies.

7. Enjoy.

Recipe 26: Traditional Tom Yum

Love to make a new soup? Try this one now.

Preparation Time: 20 mins

Yield: 4

Ingredient List:

- 6 cups chicken broth
- 2-3 stalks lemongrass, minced
- 2-3 kaffir lime leaves
- 3-4 cloves of garlic, minced
- 1 tsp. ginger, grated
- 1 red chili, minced
- 1 cup shiitake mushrooms, sliced
- 1 lime, juiced
- 2 tbsp. fish sauce
- 1 tbsp. soy sauce
- 12-14 medium shrimp
- 1 tsp. sugar
- ¼ cup coriander

HHHHHHHHHHHHHHHHHHHHHHHHHHHHHH

Instructions:

1. In a saucepan add chicken broth and let to boil.

2. Add in lemongrass, let to boil.

3. Now add in garlic, ginger, sugar, chili, fish sauce, mushrooms, lime juice, and soy sauce cook for 3-4 minutes.

4. Add in shrimp and simmer for few minutes.

5. Stir in coconut milk on lower heat.

6. Ladle soup in serving bowls and top with coriander.

Recipe 27: Five Spice Soup

Do you love a little sweet a little hot flavor of soup? Then make this one.

Preparation Time: 40 mins

Yield: 4

Ingredient List:

- 3 Tbsp. Oil
- 2 Pound Chicken Drumsticks
- 6-7 Cups Water
- 2-3 Cloves Garlic
- 1 Tsp. Coriander Seed
- ½ Tsp. White Pepper
- 3 Boiled Eggs
- 1 tbsp. Five Spice Powder
- 5 tbsp. Black Soy Sauce
- 4 tbsp. Soy Sauce
- 2 tbsp. Sugar
- 2 tsp. Salt
- 1 cup Extra-firm tofu
- 5 Thai Chile Peppers
- ¼ Cup Onion, chopped
- ¼ Cup Cilantro, chopped
- 4 tbsp. vinegar
- 6-7 Ounces Rice Flake, boiled

HHHHHHHHHHHHHHHHHHHHHHHHHHHHHHH

Instructions:

1. Heat oil in a pot and fry chicken till golden.

2. Add in water, garlic, five spice powder, coriander seed, and black pepper, mix well.

3. Stir in soy sauce, sugar, salt, eggs, tofu and mix well. Let to boil. Lower the heat and cook for 30 minutes.

4. In a mortar and pestle add in Thai chilis and make a fine past. Combine it with vinegar and stir.

5. Drizzle soup in serving bowl with rice flakes, top with sauce, spring onions and cilantro.

6. Enjoy.

Recipe 28: Thai Seafood Soup

Add seafoods in your soup and taste it in Thai style.

Preparation Time: 28 mins

Yield: 4

Ingredient List:

- 6 cups chicken stock
- 1 stalk lemongrass, minced
- 2 kaffir lime leaves
- 4 cloves garlic, minced
- 1 tsp. galangal, grated
- 1 red chili, sliced
- handful mushrooms, sliced
- 12-14 raw shrimp
- 1 tomato, sliced
- Some bok choy, chopped
- 1 can of coconut milk
- 2 tbsp. fish sauce
- 1 tbsp. soy sauce
- Juice of 1 lime
- 1 tsp. sugar
- ¼ cup cilantro leaves

HHHHHHHHHHHHHHHHHHHHHHHHHHHHHHH

Instructions:

1. In a saucepan add chicken stock and lemongrass, let to boil.

2. Add in garlic, ginger, chili, and handful of mushrooms, let to simmer for 2-3 minutes.

3. Add in shrimp, tomato and baby bok choy.

4. Let to simmer for 3 to 4 minutes.

5. Lower down the heat and in coconut milk, fish sauce, soy sauce, fresh lime juice and sugar. Mix well.

6. Pour to serving bowls and top with coriander.

Recipe 29: Rice Shrimp Soup

Make this soup and feel like a chef.

Preparation Time: 30 mins

Yield: 3

Ingredient List:

- 2 Cups Water
- 1 Cup Thai Jasmine Rice, boiled
- 1 Cup Chinese Celery, sliced
- 1 tsp. Preserved Cabbage
- 2 tbsp. Fish Sauce
- 2 tbsp. Maggi Seasoning
- ½ tbsp. Garlic, Sliced
- Few Shiitake Mushrooms, sliced
- ½ tsp. Thai Pepper Powder
- Fried Garlic, as much required
- ½ Tsp. Radish

HHHHHHHHHHHHHHHHHHHHHHHHHHHHHHH

Instructions:

1. In a saucepan heat oil and fry garlic until crisp. Add in water and let to boil. Now add in celery slices, Maggi sauce, 1 tbsp. of fish sauce and pepper, and mix.

2. Now add in rice, cabbage, mushrooms, and leave to boil.

3. Now add in shrimp and stir to combine. Simmer for 4-5 minutes.

4. Add to serving bowl and top with fried garlic coriander leaves.

Recipe 30: Tom Yum in Coconut Water with Shrimp

This soup will give you unforgettable taste.

Preparation Time: 30 mins

Yield: 4

Ingredient List:

- 5 Cups of Coconut Water
- 2 Stalks of Lemongrass
- 3 Galangal slice, chopped
- 2 tbsp. fish sauce
- 4 tbsp. Lime Juice
- 3-4 Fresh Mushrooms, sliced
- 1 tbsp. Prik Pao
- 12-13 Large Shrimp
- 7-8 grape Tomatoes
- 1 Shallot, chopped
- 3-4 Kaffir Lime Leaves
- 4 Thai Chili Peppers
- Cilantro, for Garnish

HHHHHHHHHHHHHHHHHHHHHHHHHHHHHHH

Instructions:

1. In a soup pot add coconut water with lemongrass, galangal, chili, chopped shallot, tomatoes and kafir lime leaves, let to bring.

2. Add in mushrooms and shrimps.

3. Now add in fish sauce, prik pao and lime juice.

4. Remove from heat.

5. Add to serving bowl.

6. Garnish with cilantro.

About the Author

Angel Burns learned to cook when she worked in the local seafood restaurant near her home in Hyannis Port in Massachusetts as a teenager. The head chef took Angel under his wing and taught the young woman the tricks of the trade for cooking seafood. The skills she had learned at a young age helped her get accepted into Boston University's Culinary Program where she also minored in business administration.

Summers off from school meant working at the same restaurant but when Angel's mentor and friend retired as head chef, she took over after graduation and created classic and new dishes that delighted the diners. The restaurant flourished under Angel's culinary creativity and one customer developed more than an appreciation for Angel's food. Several months after taking over the position, the young woman met her future husband at work and they have been inseparable ever since. They still live in Hyannis Port with their two children and a cocker spaniel named Buddy.

Angel Burns turned her passion for cooking and her business acumen into a thriving e-book business. She has authored several successful books on cooking different types of dishes using simple ingredients for novices and experienced chefs alike. She is still head chef in Hyannis Port and says she will probably never leave!

Author's Afterthoughts

With so many books out there to choose from, I want to thank you for choosing this one and taking precious time out of your life to buy and read my work. Readers like you are the reason I take such passion in creating these books.

It is with gratitude and humility that I express how honored I am to become a part of your life and I hope that you take the same pleasure in reading this book as I did in writing it.

Can I ask one small favour? I ask that you write an honest and open review on Amazon of what you thought of the book. This will help other readers make an informed choice on whether to buy this book.

My sincerest thanks,

Angel Burns

If you want to be the first to know about news, new books, events and giveaways, subscribe to my newsletter by clicking the link below

https://angel-burns.gr8.com

or Scan QR-code

Printed in Great Britain
by Amazon